W9-AWI-839

12/07

What if we do N**O**THING**?**

GLOBAL
WARMING

Neil Morris

**Consultant: Rob Bowden, Specialist in
Global Environmental and Social Issues**

WORLD ALMANAC® LIBRARY

Please visit our web site at: www.garethstevens.com
For a free color catalog describing World Almanac® Library's list of
high-quality books and multimedia programs, call 1-800-542-2595 (USA)
or 1-800-387-3178 (Canada). Gareth Stevens Publishing's fax: (877) 542-2596

Library of Congress Cataloging-in-Publication Data

Morris, Neil, 1946-
    Global warming / Neil Morris.
        p. cm. – (What if we do nothing?)
    Includes bibliographical references and index.
    ISBN-10: 0-8368-7755-1   ISBN-13: 978-0-8368-7755-7 (lib. bdg.)
    ISBN-10: 0-8368-8155-9   ISBN-13: 978-0-8368-8155-4 (softcover)
    1. Global warming–Juvenile literature. I. Title.
QC981.8.G56M674   2006
363.738'74–dc22   2006030444

First published in 2007 by
World Almanac® Library
An Imprint of Gareth Stevens Publishing
1 Reader's Digest Rd.
Pleasantville, NY 10570-7000 USA

Copyright © 2007 by World Almanac® Library.

Produced by Arcturus Publishing Limited
Editor: Jenni Rainford
Designer: Peta Phipps

World Almanac® Library editorial direction: Valerie J. Weber
World Almanac® Library editor: Leifa Butrick
World Almanac® Library art direction: Tammy West
World Almanac® Library graphic design: Charlie Dahl
World Almanac® Library production: Jessica Yanke and Robert Kraus

Picture credits: CORBIS: 4 (NASA/Corbis), 8 (James L. Amos/CORBIS), 11 and cover
(Hans Strand/CORBIS), 12 (Torleif Svensson/CORBIS), 15 (Roger Wood/CORBIS), 19
(NOAA/ZUMA/CORBIS), 20 (Rob Bowden/ EASI-Images), 23 (Scott T. Smith/CORBIS),
24 and cover (Nic Bothma/epa/CORBIS), 29 (Franz Marc Frei/CORBIS), 35 (Ed Kashi/CORBIS),
36 (Klaus Hackenberg/zefa/CORBIS), 39 (Yann Arthus-Bertrand/CORBIS), 40 (Jon Hicks/CORBIS),
43 (Da Silva Peter/CORBIS Sygma), 44 (CHRISTINNE MUSCHI/Reuters/CORBIS). FLPA: 30
(Michael and Patricia Fogden/Minden Pictures/FLPA). Rex Features: 7 (Image Source/Rex
Features). TopFoto: 16 (Topfoto), 27 (UNEP/Topfoto), 32 and cover (AP/Topfoto).

Printed in the United States of America

2 3 4 5 6 7 8 9 10 09 08 07

Contents

CHAPTER 1

Changing Climate

It is March 2020. World leaders and their advisors and officials on the environment have gathered in Tokyo for an important summit meeting. They have traveled to the world's largest city, but the presidents, prime ministers, and officials are not there to talk about the world's expanding population or urban development. They have come to discuss what the nations of the world can do to limit a problem with serious consequences everywhere. The issue under discussion is global warming.

Many years earlier, after countless meetings about global warming, the United Nations held an Earth Summit in Rio de Janeiro in 1992. Five years later, many of the world's representatives met in Kyoto, Japan, and many nations signed an agreement called the Kyoto Protocol to work toward slowing down global warming. This agreement came into effect in 2005, and by the beginning of the following year, 163 countries had ratified it.

What is Global Warming?

Global warming is a gradual increase in the temperature of Earth. Scientists believe that Earth's average temperature has gone up and down over millions of years. For example, during several glacial periods, or ice ages, many parts of the world were much colder than they are now. These periods alternated with shorter periods when the ice melted, and the climate was generally warmer. The last ice age ended ten to twenty thousand years ago.

This satellite image of planet Earth shows how it is lit by the Sun. The Sun's energy gives us light and heat. Without it, life on Earth would not be possible.

Natural forces caused the dramatic changes in climate; humans in prehistoric or ancient times had no influence on it. Experts think, however, that the rise in temperature in recent times—especially in the late twentieth and early twenty-first centuries—has been influenced or even caused by human activities.

Polluting Our World

During the last century, people all over the world have burned more and more fossil fuels—coal, oil, and natural gas. These fuels are nonrenewable; the limited supply will eventually run out. Fossil fuels also release pollutants, including carbon dioxide and other gases, that contribute to global warming.

The problem is that people in most regions of the world depend on fossil fuels for their energy needs. Power stations use them to make electricity, and cars and other vehicles use them as their main source of power. In 1997, Kyoto delegates concentrated on getting nations to agree to reduce the amount of harmful gases released into the atmosphere by fossil fuels. By 2020, they will know whether they achieved the effect they hoped for—a true reduction in global emissions of greenhouse gases into the Earth's atmosphere and, ultimately, a limit to global warming.

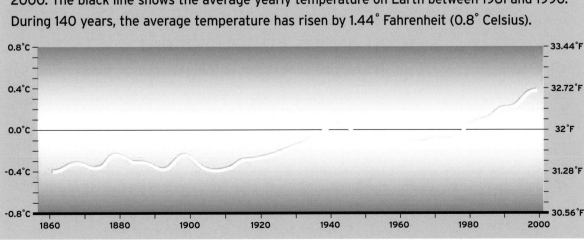

GLOBAL RISE IN TEMPERATURE

The red line on this chart shows the average yearly temperature on Earth between 1860 and 2000. The black line shows the average yearly temperature on Earth between 1961 and 1990. During 140 years, the average temperature has risen by 1.44° Fahrenheit (0.8° Celsius).

Source: Intergovernmental Panel on Climate Change

The Greenhouse Effect

The Sun's rays heat Earth's land and sea. More than one-third of the Sun's energy bounces back off the Earth's surface, however, like light reflected by a mirror, and moves back through the atmosphere toward space. Water vapor, certain gases, and particles in the atmosphere prevent the Sun's energy from escaping by absorbing some of the heat. This process is similar to the way glass traps heat inside a greenhouse, keeping it warm. For this reason, we call the action of these gases in the atmosphere the greenhouse effect.

The natural greenhouse effect makes a big difference to the temperature of our planet. Without it, the average temperature of the Earth's surface today would be about 0°F (–18°C). With the blanketing effect of the greenhouse gases, however, the actual average temperature is about 59°F (15°C)—comfortable for humans to exist.

THE MAIN GREENHOUSE GASES

Gas	Source
Carbon Dioxide (CO_2)	Found in nature, but burning any substance that contains carbon, such as coal, oil, or wood, releases CO_2.
Methane (CH_4)	The main component of natural gas. Landfill waste sites, livestock farms, and rice paddies also release it; it absorbs twenty-three times as much heat as CO_2.
Nitrous Oxide (N_2O)	Found in nature, but industry and agriculture also release it.
Ozone (O_3)	Found mostly in the upper atmosphere (the ozone layer), but also found in the lower atmosphere
Water Vapor	The biggest contributor to the natural greenhouse effect
Halocarbons	Synthetic chemicals that include a group of chlorofluorocarbons (CFCs), which used to be found in refrigerators, aerosols, and packaging materials, and the less destructive hydrochlorofluorocarbons (HCFCs)
Sulphur Hexafluoride (SF_6)	Produced in some industrial processes and mainly used in the electronics industry for insulation

Human Action

The greenhouse effect has been working for millions of years, long before human beings existed on Earth. In recent years, however, our increasing use of fossil fuels and greater industrialization has released much larger quantities of greenhouse gas into the atmosphere. This increase has upset the natural balance and created what scientists call an enhanced greenhouse effect. The effect is stronger, trapping more of the Sun's energy and causing global warming.

The most important greenhouse gas is carbon dioxide (CO_2), which animals produce naturally as they convert food into energy. On Earth, plants need carbon dioxide to live and grow, just as we need the oxygen that they give off. Burning fossil fuels for energy, however, and cutting down forests for urban development also give off large amounts of carbon dioxide. Scientists estimate that CO_2 has caused up to 70 percent of the enhanced greenhouse effect.

This oil refinery turns crude oil into gasoline and many other substances. During this process, carbon dioxide and other harmful gases are released into the atmosphere.

WHAT WOULD YOU DO?

You Are in Charge

You are a government official addressing a climate conference. You have discussed some action points. What would you suggest all countries do first?

- Set a target for reducing emission of greenhouse gases.
- Concentrate on reducing the emissions of carbon dioxide.
- Bring in programs to stop forests being cut down.
- Increase the use of renewable energy sources, such as wind, water, and solar power.
- Give incentives to people to use less energy by buying cars that use less gasoline and by using public transportation.

See the discussion on page 47 for suggestions.

CHAPTER 2

Icy Meltdown

Tulugaq was born in an Inuit community in 1980. He is forty years old now, and he looks back at how much the community on Baffin Island in the Canadian territory of Nunavut has changed since he was a boy. Now, in 2020, the winter is shorter, the ice is thinner, and he has to work much harder. Global warming has affected his traditional way of making a living, and it is more difficult to find the seals that his family has hunted for centuries. Tulugaq and his wife sell soapstone carvings of seals, bears, and caribou to tourists. Tulugaq wonders whether his children will stay in this community or even in their Inuit homeland.

Arctic Effects

Scientists have recorded the effects of global warming in the Arctic region around the North Pole for many years. These effects are easy to see. As the region warms up, the ice melts, becoming thinner in some places and disappearing altogether in others. Centuries ago, when explorers searched for a route from Europe to Asia, they tried to sail through the Bering Strait from the Arctic to the Pacific Ocean. For hundreds of years, thick ice prevented them from sailing through. In 1879, Swedish captain Nils Nordenskjöld successfully sailed through the Northeast Passage across the top of Siberia and the Bering Strait. Today, Russian icebreakers keep the channel free of ice so that ships can pass

The Greenland ice sheet is melting. Experts predict that it may take one thousand years for the sheet to disappear completely.

through. According to the Office of Naval Research, the Northeast Passage and the Northwest Passage across the top of Canada will be free of ice all year round by 2020.

Polar Ice Mass

Global warming is melting the Arctic ice on both land and sea. More than two-thirds of the Arctic Ocean is frozen all year round, but since 1980, this polar ice mass has been getting smaller by 9 percent per decade. That is nearly 1 percent each year. The ice mass is still up to 164 feet (50 meters) thick in some places, but scientists say it has thinned by between 15 and 40 percent since the mid-1970s.

On Land

Arctic ice is also melting on land, including the great ice sheet that covers about four-fifths of the world's largest island, Greenland. The ice is up to 2 miles (3.2 kilometers) thick in places, but research shows that it may be thinning at up to 32.8 feet (10 meters) per year, ten times faster than previously thought. Higher temperatures may affect Arctic permafrost, too. At the moment, this permanently frozen ground covers more than 3.8 million square miles (10 million sq km). By 2020 one-quarter of this area may no longer be permafrost.

This map shows the projected changes in Arctic sea ice.

KEY

Observed ice extent in 2002

Predicted ice extent by 2030

Predicted ice extent by 2060

Predicted ice extent by 2090

Source: based on a map produced by the Arctic Climate Impact Assessment

Albedo Effect

The Arctic region may be warming up more than other parts of the world because of the albedo effect, which refers to a surface's power to reflect light. Snow and ice are white, and so they reflect up to 90 percent of the sunlight that falls on them, compared with 45 percent that falls on a sandy desert, 20 percent for green fields, and just 3.5 percent for oceans. Our planet's average albedo is 39 percent—less than half that of the polar regions.

As ice melts, it exposes darker land or sea, which is less reflective and so absorbs more heat. As the land heats up, more ice at the edges melts, and more land or sea is exposed, and the cycle continues, building up over a period of years. It is impossible to stop. According to 2005 forecasts, the Arctic region could warm three times as much as the rest of the world in the next few decades.

Indigenous People

Climate change affects everyone, but it is particularly important to the people of the Arctic. In 1996, the eight Arctic nations—Canada, Denmark (for Greenland and the Faroe Islands), Finland, Iceland, Norway, Russia, Sweden, and the United States (for Alaska)—formed an Arctic Council to protect their environment. The council represents the interests of about 4 million people, including the Inuit of Greenland, Canada, Alaska, and Russia and the Saami (or Lapps) of northern Norway, Sweden, and Finland. Part of the Council's work is to keep monitoring the Arctic

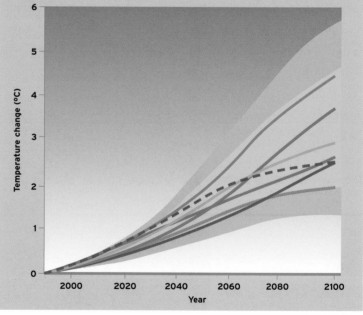

PROJECTED INCREASE IN WORLD TEMPERATURE

The range of curving lines shows how scientists' predictions vary according to how much greenhouse gas gets into the atmosphere. The lowest curve is based on little or no increase, and the upper curves on higher increases. By 2020 the temperature might go up by between 32.54°F (0.3°C) and 33.44°F (0.8°C), and by 2100, by between 34.52°F (1.4°C) and 42.44°F (5.8°C). The dotted line shows the average prediction.

Source: Intergovernmental Panel on Climate Change

environment to see how it is affected by global warming. Scientists constantly check the coverage and thickness of ice, changes in temperature, and the health and movement of Arctic animals.

If the world warmed up so much that the Arctic ice melted completely, polar bears could be extinct within one hundred years.

Living on the Pack Ice

Polar bears live only in the Arctic, where they feed mainly on seals. They have always followed the ice as it moves and retreats during the summer. They hunt seals by looking for holes in the ice where the seals come up for air. When the pack ice breaks up, polar bears swim to floating islands of ice and pounce on seals resting there. Polar bears could be greatly affected if global warming causes the reduction in sea ice that many experts predict. If the ice continues to melt at current rates, polar bears may have to change their way of life to survive.

Bears in the southern limits of the Arctic, such as Hudson Bay, are most at risk. Some experts have suggested that the bears could adapt to a less icy habitat. They could become more like brown bears in Alaska that hunt salmon in rivers and streams and small mammals on land. Others fear that they could simply die out.

Frozen Continent

The difference between the Arctic and the frozen continent of Antarctica is that most Antarctic ice lies on top of land. The ice cap is up to 3 miles (4.8 km) thick in places. The Antarctic ice sheets are so huge that more than two-thirds of the world's freshwater is locked up in its ice. The continent has no indigenous people, but a resident population of international scientists use Antarctica as an important base for studying changes in the climate.

The scientists have found that ice in the western part of Antarctica is thinning at a rate of about 4 inches (10 centimeters) per year. Owing to rising temperatures, in some places it is thinning at a rate of 13 feet (4 m) per year. Some of this thinning may be caused by volcanic heat rising up beneath the rock on which the ice rests. In

This photo shows snow and ice on top of Mount Kilimanjaro, Africa's highest mountain. It lies in Tanzania near the equator. The mountain has lost one-third of its ice in the past twelve years, and scientists believe that by 2020 its icy cap may have totally melted.

2002, a large part of the Larsen ice shelf, at the edge of the Antarctic Peninsula, broke up completely in just a little more than a month. Because of this occurence, glaciers that make their way to the sea in this region flowed up to six times faster. A scientist at the National Snow and Ice Data Center said, "If anyone was waiting to find out whether Antarctica would respond quickly to climate warming, I think the answer is yes."

The World's Glaciers

Glaciers are found in many other parts of the world, especially in high mountain ranges. When Glacier National Park in the Rocky Mountains of northern Montana was made into a national park in 1910, it had about 150 glaciers. Because of rising temperatures during the twentieth century, it now has thirty-seven named glaciers, and they have all shrunk dramatically in recent decades. During that time, for example, the park's Sperry Glacier has shrunk from an area of more than 1 square mile (3 sq km) to less than 0.4 square mile (1 sq km). A similar situation has been found in the European Alps and the South American Andes.

Shorter Winters

Scientists have discovered that winters have become shorter in recent decades, which may be another result of global warming. Records show that a lake in Wisconsin froze over for 119 days of the year more than a century ago, whereas in the early twenty-first century, it froze for just eighty days. The world's deepest lake—Lake Baikal in Russia—freezes over for twenty-three days fewer than it did one hundred years ago.

WHAT WOULD YOU DO?

You Are in Charge
You represent a local community of indigenous people in one of the Arctic countries. You have an appointment with the environment official of your country. Explain how global warming concerns you. What evidence could you use to convince the official to take the issue seriously?

CHAPTER 3

Rising Seas

Like millions of their fellow Bangladeshis, Shamsur, his wife Jakia, and their family are rice farmers. Twenty years ago, they used to get three crops a year from their small plot, using the seasonal rains to their advantage. Now, in 2020, times are very hard: Their paddy fields are constantly under too much water, and the water contains too much salt from the sea. Shamsur and Jakia have moved their plot several times, but they do not know whether they will get permission from the agricultural authorities to move it again. The authorities know that Bangladesh is fast running out of usable farmland, making it difficult to feed its 210 million people.

A Global Issue

A warmer world has always meant rising sea levels. About 130,000 years ago, before the beginning of the last ice age, world temperature was a little higher than today—about 3.6°F (2°C) warmer. At that time, the average sea level was 16 or 20 feet (5 or 6 m) higher than today. About 18,000 years ago, however, ice cover was very thick, and the sea level was more than 328 feet (100 m) lower than it is now. The Atlantic Ocean and North Sea were so low that Britain was joined by dry land to continental Europe.

PROJECTED RISE IN SEA LEVEL

The range of curving lines shows varying predictions according to different increases in greenhouse gas emissions. The lowest curve is based on little or no increase, and the upper curves on higher increases. By 2020 sea level might go up by between .8 inch (2 centimeters) and 4 inches (10 cm), and by 2100 by between 4 inches (10 cm) and 3 feet (90 cm). The red dotted line shows the average prediction.

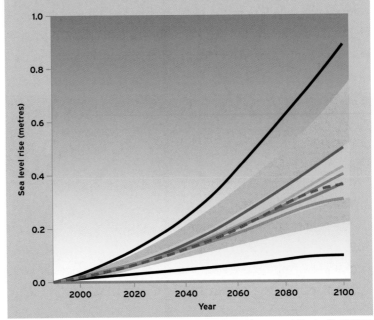

Source: Intergovernmental Panel on Climate Change

An Egyptian man rides his donkey across the Nile River Delta. If sea levels rise as scientists warn, this area is at great risk of total flooding from the Mediterranean Sea.

Warm water is less dense than cold water, so global warming makes the oceans expand. Much more important, melting ice turns to water, so the warming of the two polar regions and of the glaciers around the world will potentially have a huge impact on sea level.

Living near Low-Lying Coasts and River Deltas

According to an estimate by the National Geographic Society, more than 100 million people live on land that is less than 3 feet (1 m) above present sea level. That land will disappear if the sea rises by 3 feet (1 m). According to current forecasts, it appears that the sea might rise as much as 4 inches (10 cm) by 2020 and as much as 3 feet (90 cm) by 2100. What people living in the twenty-second century can expect is more difficult to predict.

The world's river deltas are densely populated; these areas may be the hardest hit if sea levels rise. The Nile River Delta in northern Egypt and the Mississippi River Delta in the southern United States are particularly vulnerable. Two other factors could affect the Ganges River Delta of Bangladesh if the sea level rises there. The land there is already subsiding because of land movements. Also, vast quantities of groundwater are being removed for drinking and irrigation. Experts say that if the sea rises near Bangladesh, the effects could be the same as a rise in the sea level of 3 feet (1 m) by 2050.

Low-Lying Islands

About half a million people live on groups of small, low-lying islands around the world. Some of the world's low-lying islands have already experienced the effects of the sea levels rising, and many people have been forced to move away from the coast or even leave their islands. In the Pacific island country of Tuvalu, for example, where the sea level rose 8 to 12 inches (20 to 30 cm) during the twentieth century, people began leaving the small islands in 2001.

The Maldives consist of about twelve hundred small coral islands that form a chain more than 466 miles (750 km) long in the Indian Ocean, to the southwest of India. Two hundred of them are inhabited. Their total land area now is only 115 square miles (298 sq km)—less than one-third the size of New York City. Natural barrier reefs

On the low-lying Maldives, fishing and tourism provide most of the islanders' income. As sea levels rise and land disappears, however, fewer people will be able to live on the islands, and tourists may no longer be able to visit them.

surround many of the island atolls, but they will not be able to protect them from the rising sea. The highest point on the Maldives is currently just 8 feet (2.4 m) above sea level.

The disastrous tsunami of December 26, 2004, showed the Maldivians the reality of what life might be like if sea levels rise. Forty percent of their land was under water at some point. Fortunately, most of the islanders live in Male, the nation's capital, which is protected by a high sea wall. Nevertheless, homes on twenty inhabited islands were completely destroyed, fifteen thousand Maldivians lost their homes, and eighty-two were killed.

An increase in sea levels would be a gradual process, unlike a tsunami, however. It would be probably not lead to such death and destruction. A rise in sea levels remains a serious threat, however, and the government has launched a Safe Islands project, picking out five main islands that they will try to protect from rising seas.

Pacific Islands

Rising sea levels also threaten many of the thousands of small Pacific islands. These land masses include the Marshall Islands; a 1.6-foot (0.5-m) rise in sea level would submerge more than three-quarters of the country's 70-square-mile (181-sq-km) area.

People on the Marshall Islands and the Maldives are sharing ideas with other island groups, such as in the Bahamas in the Atlantic. They are developing early warning systems in case of a sudden rise in sea levels, and they are looking at ways to help islanders protect their homes or relocate to other areas. In 1990, during a World Climate Conference in Geneva, the islands formed the Alliance of Small Island States (AOSIS), which now has more than forty members. At one of their regular meetings, the delegate for the Caribbean island of Saint Lucia said they had to take action on rising sea levels now: "If we wait for the proof, the proof will kill us."

What happens to the world's low-lying areas will depend on how much and how quickly world temperatures rise. Although the world's climate does go through natural periods of warming, the rate of current warming appears to be at least partly due to human influence.

TWENTY HOTTEST YEARS ON RECORD

The records of annual temperatures, which date back as far as 1880, show that eighteen of the hottest years on record have occurred since the mid-1980s.

Rank	Year
=1	2005
=1	1998
3	2002
4	2003
5	2004
6	2001
7	1997
8	1990
9	1995
10	1999
11	2000
12	1991
13	1987
14	1988
15	1994
16	1983
17	1996
18	1944
19	1989
20	1993

Source: Union of Concerned Scientists

Flood Defences

In Europe, figures show that the sea has risen by about 6 inches (15 cm) over the past two hundred years. This rise has had a big effect on countries such as the Netherlands, which is one of the Low Countries (along with Belgium and Luxembourg). About half of the Netherlands' land lies below sea level. For centuries, the Dutch have built banks and dikes along their coast to keep out the sea and have reclaimed the land by draining seawater from flooded areas.

In 1953, huge waves crashed over the dikes and flooded a large coastal region. The Dutch government then built the 4.35-mile- (7-k-) long Dutch Sea Barrier, a series of strong dams with concrete piers and steel gates that allow water to enter when the gates are open. The gates can be closed during very high tides or severe storms. The Dutch also drained some areas, called polders, using windmills or pumps to transfer the water into drainage canals that led to rivers and back to the sea. Some polders are more than 20 feet (6 m) below sea level. Other countries can learn a great deal from the Dutch experience, but poorer countries, such as Bangladesh or the Maldives, would need financial help to build such defenses.

Disaster Strikes

The Asian tsunami of December 2004 destroyed the sea defenses of many areas around the Indian Ocean and took the lives of many thousands of people. In 2005, during Hurricane Katrina, a surge of water struck the levee protecting New Orleans from Lake Pontchartrain on the Gulf Coast. The storm passed 20 miles (32 km) east of downtown New Orleans, destroying many buildings, flooding more than three-quarters of the city, and killing more than thirteen hundred people. The damage was caused by the surge of water and the destruction of coastal and river levees more than by the winds. Katrina was a clear warning that the potential increase in sea levels will have a dramatic effect on the lives of people living in such low-lying areas.

WHAT WOULD YOU DO?

You Are in Charge
You are an official working for the international community, and you are addressing a seminar on global accountability. Which nations would you argue should take responsibility for their CO_2 emissions? Should those nations help to pay the cost of protecting low-lying areas around the world against rising sea levels?

Tropical cyclones (generally called hurricanes in the western Atlantic; typhoons in the western Pacific; and cyclones in the Indian Ocean) form over warm oceans with a water temperature of at least 80°F (27°C). Many scientists believe that warmer oceans will lead to more tropical cyclones, and their predictions already are evident in the western Atlantic, including the Caribbean Sea and Gulf of Mexico.

The year 2005 broke all records for storms in the western Atlantic region. There were twenty-seven named storms (twice the recent average), fourteen hurricanes, and seven major hurricanes (twice the recent average). Of the seven major hurricaines, three reached category-5 status—the highest level, with wind speeds of more than 156 miles (251 km) per hour—including Hurricane Katrina.

This satellite image shows Hurricane Katrina as it moved toward the Gulf Coast in August 2005. The calm eye in the middle of the hurricane is clearly visible, with thick clouds whirling around it.

CHAPTER 4

Human Health

It is 2020, and Emma, a successful British TV producer, has won an award for best sports documentary. The presentation ceremony is being held in Beijing. Emma has traveled all over the world making documentaries and is surprised to discover that she will now need to take antimalaria tablets and use mosquito spray and a net over her bed for her trip to northern China. Malaria is advancing ever northward to previously unaffected regions.

Since human health depends on good environmental conditions and is linked to climate, experts believe that global warming will hurt human life in several different ways. Air pollution, poor soil conditions, and inadequate food and water would increase health problems and the spread of disease.

Heat Stress

Experts anticipate that rising temperatures may lead to more people becoming ill or even dying from the heat. Scientists warn that climate change may already be causing 160,000 deaths a year and that heat-related fatalities could double by 2020.

In the summer of 2003, about thirty-five thousand people died as a result of a record heat wave in Europe. The death toll was highest in France, where nearly fifteen thousand people died. It was the hottest August on record in the northern hemisphere. Earlier in the year, it had been even hotter in India. In May 2003, temperatures there soared to 120°F (49°C) and claimed more than sixteen hundred lives. People brought up in hot countries are generally more tolerant of heat waves. Scientists say that people in London, especially the elderly, start to suffer at 72°F (22°C), while in the Greek capital of Athens, heat-related health problems begin at 79°F (26°C).

This farmer in Rajasthan, India, is plowing dry scrubland. Animals and plants that make good food have difficulty surviving on such land. Higher temperatures and drought would affect farmers all over the world in both rich and poor regions.

Heat stress mainly affects old, very young, or chronically ill people. Out of more than two thousand people who died in the 2003 heat wave in Britain, 85 percent were seventy-five and older. Scientists point out that hotter summers will be followed by milder winters, which may lead to fewer deaths due to extremes of cold. Nevertheless, according to the Earth Policy Institute of Washington, D.C., heat waves claim more lives each year than floods, tornadoes, and hurricanes.

World Food Supply

Many people in developing countries farm the land and grow their own food, but often they simply cannot produce enough. The result is that at least 800 million people (12 percent of the world's population) are starving. If growing conditions become more difficult in developing countries because the climate becomes hotter and drier, farmers will find life even more difficult. Aid agencies are trying to combat this problem by helping people improve their own farming techniques.

Experts predict that by 2020 developing countries will depend even more on richer nations for staple cereal crops than they do now. The cereal deficit in developing countries is likely to be three times as high as it was in 1988. Unfair trade laws allow rich, industrialized countries to control the world food network, help their own producers, and keep down the price they pay for imported food. If global warming adds to the difficulties of food production, the rich nations will have to do more to help poor regions.

Experts predict that by 2020, developed countries will increase their production of cereals and the amount they can export to other countries. As the "net supply" of developing countries shows, these nations will need those cereal crops.

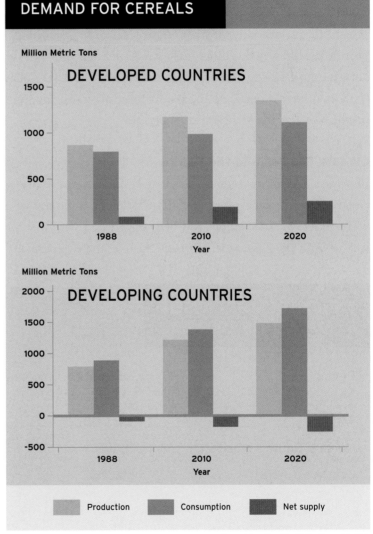

PROJECTED SUPPLY AND DEMAND FOR CEREALS

Million Metric Tons

DEVELOPED COUNTRIES

Million Metric Tons

DEVELOPING COUNTRIES

Production   Consumption   Net supply

Source: International Food Policy Research Institute

Increased Spread of Disease

A hotter climate may increase the risk of catching certain diseases. Hot weather helps bacteria breed, so more people could come down with food poisoning. Serious waterborne bacterial diseases, such as cholera and typhoid, might also increase, especially if global warming leads to wetter as well as warmer conditions in parts of the world, such as Bangladesh, that are already vulnerable to these diseases.

Diseases that are spread by certain kinds of mosquitoes and other insects—malaria, dengue fever, yellow fever, and encephalitis—could become more common if warmer temperatures allow these insects to survive outside their native regions. According to the World Health Organization, malaria is one of the world's most devastating diseases; more people suffer from malaria today than from any other disease. As the population increases, the number of people affected and at risk also increases.

Climate Studies and the Future

In Africa and other regions stricken by malaria, a World Health Organization project called Roll Back Malaria is providing people with sprays for their homes and bed nets treated with insecticide as well as with new antimalarial drugs. Also, climate experts are using

ANNUAL DEATHS CAUSED BY MALARIA IN 2002-03			
Region	**No. of Deaths**	**% of World Total**	**No. of Deaths of Children under 5**
Africa	1,136,000	89	802,000
North & South America	1,000	0.1	1,000
Southeast Asia	65,000	5	12,000
Europe	0	0	0
Eastern Mediterranean	59,000	5	37,000
Western Pacific	11,000	0.9	1,000
TOTAL	1,272,000	100	853,000

Source: World Health Organization

computer models of changing weather patterns to predict outbreaks of malaria up to five months in advance. In Botswana, the National Malaria Control Program has developed an early warning system. In neighboring South Africa, scientists believe that if nothing is done, the numbers of those at high risk of contracting malaria will quadruple by 2020.

Whatever happens in terms of global warming, the future of all these diseases, including malaria, may vary greatly in different parts of the world. The number of cases will depend on many other factors, including the wealth and public health system of any particular region.

Water Problems

Clean fresh water is essential to good health, so scientists are looking at how global warming might affect the world's water cycle. A rise in sea levels may cause salt water to enter groundwater reserves and contaminate some freshwater supplies. At the same time, dry areas are expected to become drier.

The term *water stress* refers to the proportion of available freshwater that is withdrawn for use. The World Water Council defines withdrawal of 10 percent as *low water stress*, 20 percent withdrawal is *mid water stress*, 40 percent is *high water stress,* and 80 percent is *very high water stress.* Many countries already suffer from water stress, particularly in North Africa and southwestern and central Asia. In the 1990s, about 1.7 billion people lived in mid- to very high-stressed regions. This number is expected to increase to about 5 billion (nearly 60 percent of the estimated world population) by 2025.

This person is wearing mosquito-proof headgear to keep the insects away from his skin. When mosquitoes bite people to feed on their blood and moisture, they can infect them with malaria.

This Sudanese girl
is carrying water
from an inter-
national aid camp.
Safe drinking water
is a precious
resource throughout
northern Africa. As
the world's
population grows,
demand for water
increases, so it
may become even
more scarce.

During the second half of the twentieth century, worldwide water use tripled. In North America and Japan, people in residential areas used an average of 93 gallons (350 liters) a day; in Europe, the figure was 53 gallons (200 l); but in sub-Saharan Africa, the figure was just 2.6 to 5.3 gallons (10 to 20 l). In 2003, the World Water Forum decided that the aim for 2020 should be 10.5 gallons (40 l) per person, per day worldwide.

Today, more than one in six people across the world lack access to safe drinking water. Between 2000 and 2020, the need for water will grow by about 26 percent. By 2020, experts predict, the world's population will reach more than 8 billion, and, by then, up to two-thirds of the world's people may face shortages of clean freshwater. We do not know, however, exactly how global warming will affect this situation, and, in some regions, it may lead to more rainfall.

Shrinking Lakes

During the 1960s, Lake Chad covered an area of 8,880 square miles (23,000 sq km) and spread across the borders of Chad, Niger, Nigeria, and Cameroon in Africa. By 2005, it had shrunk to just 347 square miles (900 sq km), and its shores were all within the country of Chad. It has always been a seasonal lake, however, growing in size during the rainy season from July to September, and it was always shallow, with many parts clogged by reeds and other plants.

The debate on global warming is complex. Scientists who believe that global warming is a serious threat argue that the changes in the world's lake sizes are hard evidence of climate change. Other scientists argue that poor land and irrigation management caused lakes to shrink. Many scientists believe that thousands of years ago, for example, Lake Chad was a vast inland sea, but they have also found evidence that it may have dried up several times in the past thousand years. These changes would have been mainly the result of natural variations in the climate. Since the 1960s, however, the lake has received less water because its feeder rivers are used for irrigation of nearby cotton fields.

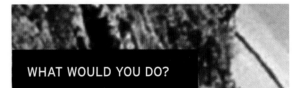

WHAT WOULD YOU DO?

You Are in Charge
As an up-and-coming politician, you represent a region that is planning to build a large river dam to supply domestic water and hydroelectricity. Your constituents ask you how global warming might affect the river and their water supplies in years to come. How would you reply?

Endangering Species

It is 2020, and Stef has just joined the Great Barrier Reef Marine Park Authority (GBRMPA), which is celebrating its forty-fifth birthday. She is proud to work for an organization that is responsible for the care and development of a UNESCO World Heritage site, Australia's beautiful coral reefs. Stef's job is to check the permits of tour guides, give advice on any problems, and make sure they obey the regulations. Twenty years ago, the Marine Park had 820 tour guides and 1.8 million visitors to the reef. Now the figures are much higher, but, at the same time, some of the reefs are dying because of rising sea temperatures.

Dwindling Biodiversity

Global warming has an effect on ecosystems, so the animals and plants that live within each habitat will begin to suffer. Scientists are concerned that global warming will lead to a decline in biodiversity—the variety of plant and animal life in a particular

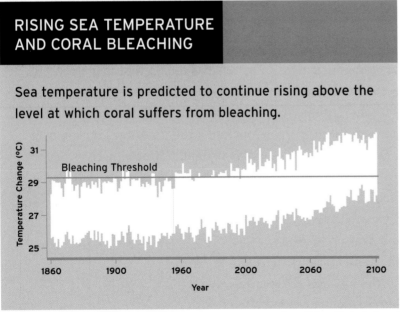

RISING SEA TEMPERATURE AND CORAL BLEACHING

Sea temperature is predicted to continue rising above the level at which coral suffers from bleaching.

Source: Marine and Freshwater Research

habitat. Conservationists warn that some species that are endangered now may even face extinction in the not-too-distant future.

The Intergovernmental Panel on Climate Change lists some species as being particularly threatened by global warming:

- mountain gorilla of Rwanda, Democratic Republic of the Congo, and Uganda
- amphibians of Central and South America
- spectacled bear of South America
- forest birds of Tanzania
- Bengal tiger of the Sundarban wetlands in India and Bangladesh
- polar bear of the Arctic
- penguins of the Antarctic

Coral Bleaching

Global warming is already having a great effect on the world's coral reefs. We see it in Australia's Great Barrier Reef, which is a series of coral reefs that stretches for more than 1,430 miles (2,300 km) along the Queensland coast. This collection of reefs has more than four hundred types of coral. These animals are coelenterates called polyps, and they make the limestone skeletons that build up the reef. The polyps cannot exist without algae that live in their tissue, however, and it is these algae that are specially affected by climate change. A rise in sea temperature of 1.8°F (1°C) causes the polyps to expel the algae and thereby lose their color. This process is called bleaching, and it generally happens when the water is about 85°F (29.5°C). The average sea temperature around the Great Barrier Reef has been rising since the end of the 1990s and will probably continue rising this century. If the sea temperature increases by 5.4°F (3°C), the coral will die.

Rising sea temperatures can also lead to coral diseases, which can affect the 1,500 species of fish and other marine animals that live among the reefs. In 2002, the GBRMPA started a program that coordinates guides, researchers, and the public to report cases of bleaching.

Just like the Great Barrier Reef, this coral reef off the Ryukyu Islands of Japan has been affected by bleaching in recent years.

Penguin Populations

All species of penguin live in cold, southern waters, and several live and breed around the coasts of Antarctica. These flightless birds are well adapted to cold air and water, and scientists are concerned that global warming could affect them very much. On the Antarctic Peninsula, average winter temperatures have increased by nearly 9°F (5°C) in the last half century, and the seas have also warmed up. The fish, krill, and other sea creatures that penguins eat have become scarce because of the rise in temperature, resulting in a loss of food.

On small islands off Antarctica, researchers have found that since the mid-1970s the number of Adélie penguins has dropped from thirty-two thousand breeding pairs to just eleven thousand. They have also discovered that Gentoo penguins are slowly replacing the Adélies. The Gentoos are migrating toward the South Pole from places such as the Falkland Islands in search of colder waters and ice.

Wetlands

According to the Ramsar List of Wetlands of International Importance, the world's wetlands—including swamps, marshes, fens, and bogs—cover an area of about 500,000 square miles (1.3 million sq km). That is an area about twice the size of Texas. Wetlands are very important because of their biodiversity, but coastal wetlands are already being lost at a rate of up to 1.5 percent per year, due mainly to pollution and clearance for other uses, such as farming or housing. A rise in sea levels will make this worse.

Coastal salt marshes and mangrove swamps could move slowly inland, but then their retreat might place them next to human flood defenses and farmland, causing the wetlands to die out completely. Scientists have estimated that a sea level rise of 1 foot (0.3 m) could wipe out up to 43 percent of the United States' wetlands.

ESTIMATED REGIONAL AREA OF WETLANDS

The International Convention on Wetlands covers 150 countries and 1,590 wetland sites.

Region	Million Acres (Hectares)	% of total
Africa	110 (44.7)	33
Central & South America	71 (28.8)	22
Europe	53 (21.5)	16
North America	48 (19.6)	15
Asia	28 (11.3)	8
Oceania	20 (8.1)	6
total	330 (134.0)	100

Source: Ramsar Convention on Wetlands/Wetlands International

According to the National Resources Defense Council, a rise in sea level, increasing temperatures, and alterations in rainfall will combine to damage the Everglades lake-marsh area in Florida. The sea along the Florida coast appears to be rising six to ten times faster than the average rate for the region over the past three thousand years. The Everglades area covers 2,350 square miles (6,100 sq km) and supports a rich range of plants and animals. Because of the decline in their habitat size, many birds of the Everglades region are already becoming rare, including the anhinga, or snakebird, which feeds on fish by spearing them with its long bill.

The Pantanal in Brazil is an amazing mixture of rivers, freshwater lakes, shrub-dominated wetlands, and seasonally flooded forests. It contains several endangered species, including hyacinth macaws, giant otters, and marsh deer as well as numerous nesting sites for the rare Jabiru stork. It also has 260 fish species. All this diversity of life is threatened by loss of such wetlands.

Mangrove forest covers the southern part of the Everglades wetlands, where freshwater meets the salty sea. This forest makes an ideal environment for many plants and animals, but because it is low-lying, the area is vulnerable to rising sea levels.

Forests and the Carbon Cycle

The world's rain forests play an important role in regulating the global climate because trees are a major part of our planet's carbon cycle. All animals breathe carbon dioxide (CO_2) into the air. Plants, including trees, absorb this carbon dioxide to produce more food. This cycle keeps a natural balance of carbon dioxide and oxygen, as carbon moves to and from the Earth's atmosphere. As part of this process, forests, along with oceans, act as one of the planet's natural carbon storerooms. They also assist the production of rainfall. Water evaporation is higher over forests than cleared land; the water turns to vapor and rises into the air, later forming clouds and producing rain.

The golden toad of Costa Rica is now extinct. Researchers believe that these toads were killed by a fungal disease that was triggered by the changed climate of the cloud forest.

Over the last few decades, huge areas of forest have been cut down to clear the land for farming or urban development; the trees are used for timber. Much of the wood that is cut down is burned as fuel, releasing carbon dioxide into the atmosphere. At the same time, cutting down forests reduces rainfall.

Global warming cannot simply be blamed on cutting down trees, however. Forests have a lower albedo than land that has been cleared often, so they keep the surface warmer. Also, scientists have recently discovered that forests give off more methane than they once thought. Nevertheless, most scientists are convinced that deforestation contributes to global warming, while afforestation—turning land into forest—could help to limit it.

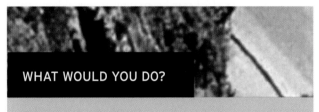

WHAT WOULD YOU DO?

You Are in Charge
You belong to an environmental group that is creating a leaflet about deforestation and how it could affect the world's climate. What examples would you use to show how we could help protect forests?

Moving Up

As the world warms up, animals and plants that are adapted to cooler climates will try to move to higher latitudes or higher altitudes. Polar bears and penguins are some examples of the first group as they move toward the North and South poles, respectively. Other animals and plants that live in the foothills or lower slopes of mountains will try to move higher up, although not all will succeed because the land will not always suit them. Cloud forest is evergreen mountainous forest, found in tropical areas, that has a low-level cloud cover. Only a small band of land—about 6,500 to 9,850 feet (2,000 to 3,000 m) above sea level—is just right for this environment of trees and plants. This kind of forest is being severely affected by global warming because in recent years, researchers have found more clouds, but they have found them forming at higher altitudes. This change is forcing plants to move higher up the mountain, where there is more cloud and it is cooler. Eventually the plants will run out of room.

The Monteverde cloud forest, in Costa Rica, is home to a variety of animals. These include howler and white-faced monkeys, snakes, frogs, moths, and thousands of tropical birds, including thirty kinds of hummingbirds. In 1999, scientists reported that they thought the golden toad that previously lived in this forest was extinct.

CHAPTER 6

Weather Warnings

The García family have built up their small coffee-growing business in Santa Teresa, 4,900 feet (1,500 m) up in the Peruvian Andes. Now, in 2020, they are benefiting from extra sales to tourists on the trail to the nearby Machu Picchu ancient Inca citadel. The older members of the family, however, live in constant fear of landslides and mudslides. They cannot forget January 1998, when terrible El Niño rains swept away their small town, destroying many homes and killing twenty-two people. Since then, they have had more scares, and the warmer and wetter the summers become, the more fearful the family grows.

One of the great unknowns is whether storms, drought, and other extreme weather conditions will increase due to global warming. Climatologists and other scientists are unsure about the future, and they do not all agree. It does seem, however, that an increase in sea temperature will affect ocean currents and the frequency of tropical storms. An increase may also cause some other hazardous weather phenomena, such as lake shrinkage, and create generally hotter, drier lands.

A stream of trucks help survivors of the 1998 El Niño mudslide in Peru make their way downhill with any possessions they can recover.

The El Niño Effect

Since the early 1980s, a climate effect in the Pacific Ocean has become more frequent and more severe. The most famous part of the effect is known as El Niño (meaning *boy child* in Spanish) because it usually begins around the time of the coming of the boy child, Jesus, at Christmas. El Niño happens when the normal easterly trade winds weaken or even reverse direction. This change in the winds causes the upper layer of warm water in the western Pacific to flow eastward toward the northern part of South America. The climate changes of El Niño cause increased rainfall and storms along the west coast of North and South America. At the other end of the globe, El Niño causes drought in Indonesia and Australia.

A strong El Niño usually occurs every three to seven years and may last for a year. Scientists often refer to it as ENSO (for El Niño–Southern Oscillation). The oscillation refers to the change between El Niño, normal conditions, and a third phenomenon called La Niña (*girl child*). During La Niña, warm surface water flows toward Asia, leaving colder deep-sea water to come to the surface near the Americas. The chart below shows how sea surface temperatures have changed in the eastern Pacific Ocean this century, starting with a period of La Niña that was followed by an El Niño episode.

The strongest El Niño conditions on record were from 1997 to 1998. They caused torrential rains, floods, and mudslides in Peru; violent storms in California; and ferocious forest fires in Indonesia because of the intensely dry conditions there.

SEA SURFACE TEMPERATURE CHANGE

Scientists use a threshold of 0.91°F (0.5°C) above or below normal sea temperature to determine El Niño and La Niña conditions. They usually call a period of five consecutive months above the threshold an El Niño episode and five months below, a La Niña episode.

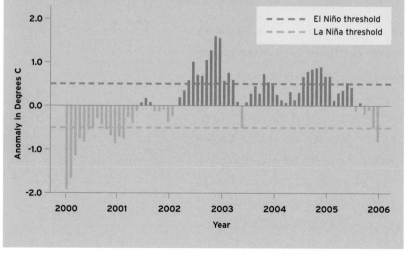

Source: US National Climatic Data Center/NESDIS/NOAA

Ocean Currents

The circulation of ocean currents acts like a giant conveyor belt, moving warm and cold water around the planet. The currents are driven by differences in water temperature and salinity (level of saltiness) so they could be altered by global warming. The Gulf Stream is a major current that takes warm water from the tropical Caribbean Sea up into the North Atlantic Ocean toward northern Europe. Westerly winds are also warmed as they cross the Gulf Stream, and they help give Western Europe milder winters than other regions in the same latitude.

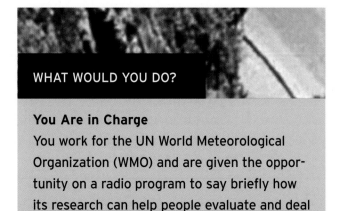

WHAT WOULD YOU DO?

You Are in Charge
You work for the UN World Meteorological Organization (WMO) and are given the opportunity on a radio program to say briefly how its research can help people evaluate and deal with the potential effects of global warming. What are the main points to put across?

Climatologists, or scientists who study weather, worry that global warming could weaken the Gulf Stream. This current depends on cool water sinking in the north and traveling south again, where it warms up, rises, and heads north. As global warming makes Arctic ice melt, the freshwater would make the ocean less salty, and therefore less dense, so that it would not sink. The circulation would weaken. Studies have shown that the Gulf Stream slowed by nearly one-third in the twelve years preceding 2005. If this trend continues, it could have a major effect on European climate, leading to colder winters, more frequent storms, and severe weather.

Deserts and Droughts

The world's deserts—defined as dry regions that receive less than 10 inches (25 cm) of rain a year—cover about one-fifth of the Earth's land area. Scientists are not sure what global warming will do to deserts. Some predict more rainfall and, therefore, more clouds and lower temperatures. Others are more worried about the problem of desertification—the process by which dry regions grow bigger, spread, and become deserts. Desertification is at least partly caused by global warming. In 1994, the United Nations set up a Convention to Combat Desertification (UNCCD), and its researchers believe that growing desertification affects one-third of the Earth's surface and the lives of more than 1 billion people.

About one-third of the world's dry lands are in Africa, with another third in Asia and the rest spread around the other continents. Chad is in an African region known as the Sahel, which lies just to the south of the Sahara Desert. Here, global warming is making the land drier. Along with other factors, such as the increase in human and livestock population and poor land management, global warming is adding to the problems of desertification.

A Forest Service helicopter deliberately starts a fire to clear the ground and stop an advancing wildfire in California. More heat means more forest fires, and hot, dry regions such as this are most at risk.

CHAPTER 7

Fuel for Transportation

There is record attendance at the 2020 International Motor Show in Geneva. This annual event has been famous since 1905 for introducing all the latest designs, prototypes, and concept cars. Things have changed, however. Instead of looking for fast new supercars or powerful four-wheel drive cars, buyers are searching for innovation in fuel use. They still want stylish vehicles with plenty of comfort and safety features, but more than anything else, they want vehicles that are both economical and environmentally friendly. Manufacturers want to please ordinary motorists and avoid high taxes, so gasoline engines are rare compared to the latest fuel-cell models.

More than one-fifth of the world's energy is used in transportation by being turned into motor power, and transportation is a big contributor to greenhouse gas emissions. The other large uses of energy are in industry and buildings. A smaller proportion of energy goes to agriculture. Scientists figure that in the early twenty-first century, about 30 percent of greenhouse gas emissions comes from transportation because most vehicles burn fossil fuels.

A motorist fills up with gasoline, which will give off exhaust gases as it burns.

Today's Fuels

For many years the main fuels for transportation have been gasoline, diesel oil, and kerosene (paraffin oil). They are all made from the same raw material—crude oil—and more than one-third of the world's oil is refined into gasoline. Every day we burn nearly 800 million gallons (3 billion l) of gasoline, mostly in cars; more than two-fifths of the gasoline is used in the United States. Diesel oil needs less refining and is used by some cars, trucks, and buses as well as by railway locomotives and ships. Jet aircraft burn kerosene.

Difficulties in Predicting the Future

Experts try to predict how much CO_2 and other greenhouse gases we will release into the atmosphere in the future. Of course, they do not know and can only make an educated guess. The Intergovernmental Panel on Climate Change uses many different future scenarios, including the number of cars on the roads, possible changes in industrial processes, and possible CO_2 emissions to forecast the future. In their figures, the number of gigatonnes (or billions of tonnes) of emissions in 2020 varies between a low of 8.8 gigatons (8 gigatonnes) and a possible high of 14.3 gigatons (13 gigatonnes). They say that by 2050, the figure could still be as low as 10 gigatons (9 gigatonnes), as shown in the table, but it could be as high as 25.3 gigatons (23 gigatonnes) if we do not change to using other fuels.

FOSSIL FUELS AND TRANSPORTATION 1990-2050

The scientists who produced these predictions used average figures, based on how they think people all over the world might use fossil fuels.

Percent of Transportation Fuel from Fossil Fuels

1990	2000	2010	2020	2030	2040	2050
97	91	81	74	63	57	52

Emissions from Fossil Fuels in Gigatonnes of Carbon

1990	2000	2010	2020	2030	2040	2050
5.8	6.9	8.0	9.2	10.7	10.6	10.0

Source: International Energy Agency/ International Institute for Applied Systems Analysis

Air Travel

Air travel presents a special problem in terms of greenhouse gas emission. Aircraft emit gases and particles high in the atmosphere, and some people suspect they are particularly damaging, especially to the ozone layer. Experts estimate that aircraft contribute about 3 percent of the CO_2 that comes from human sources. Aircraft also emit water vapor, a greenhouse gas that we sometimes see as vapor trails in the sky. The vapor increases high cloud cover, which also has a blanketing effect on the Earth's surface.

Since the beginning of the 1990s, air travel has increased by more than 5 percent every year. More aircraft, more airports, more flights, and more passengers mean more pollution. The growth figures in the chart below show passenger-miles (kilometers)—the number of passengers multiplied by the distance they fly. In 2005, the total number of passengers for the year reached 4 billion, a 6 percent increase from the previous year.

Trades, Taxes, and Offset Plans

Some people feel that airlines should pay for the damage they cause to the atmosphere and their considerable contribution to the greenhouse effect and global warming. One way to get them to pay is to include airlines in an emissions trading proposal. Authorities

SCHEDULED PASSENGER TRAFFIC IN BILLIONS OF PASSENGER-MILES (-KILOMETERS)

Area	1993	2005	%Increase
Africa	27 (43.3 km)	45.4 (73.1)	+ 68.8%
Asia/Pacific	274 (440.1)	546.5 (879.6)	+ 99.9%
Europe	310 (498.1)	566.6 (911.9)	+ 83.1%
Middle East	36 (58.4)	83 (134.0)	+ 129.5%
North America	505 (813.8)	745 (1199.3)	+ 47.4%
Latin America/Caribbean	60 (95.7)	93 (149.5)	+ 74.4%
WORLD	1,212 (1949.4)	2,079.5 (3347.4)	+ 71.7%

Source: International Civil Aviation Organization

would have to agree on a total amount of emissions, and then airlines could buy percentages of the total in the form of permits to emit CO_2. Companies could trade permits to meet emission reduction targets. Another way to make airlines pay for their emissions is to increase taxes on aviation. Ultimately, both of these plans would lead to an increase in ticket prices as the airlines pass on the costs to their customers.

Alternatively, passengers could enter an offset plan. Offset plans give people the opportunity to pay for the carbon emissions that they cause by contributing to a fund that will be used to pay for projects that combat further growth of the greenhouse effect. Some fundable projects find ways to improve energy efficiency (reducing the amount of fuel needed) or to provide renewable energy (reducing the use of fossil fuels).

If you flew to Geneva for the annual Motor Show, for example, you could calculate how much CO_2 you have to offset and, therefore, how much you have to pay. A one-way flight from New York to Geneva, for example, creates an emission of 1.92 tons (1.74 tonnes) of CO_2. A flight from Tokyo creates 3 tons (2.74 tonnes). In 2006, the offset cost for the Tokyo flight would be $100—not a lot of money on top of the fare.

Aircraft are parked at Charles de Gaulle airport, Paris, which handled nearly 54 million passengers in 2005. The world's busiest airport was in Atlanta, Georgia, with nearly 86 million passengers. Increased air traffic will add to greenhouse gas emissions.

On the Road

Cars are more popular than ever, and most of them run on gasoline or diesel fuel. These all give off CO_2, but there is a great difference between various models. A small car, for example, emits .47 liters of CO_2 per mile (113 grams per km) and travels 60 miles on every gallon (21 km on every liter) of fuel. A large car, on the other hand, emits 1.66 liters of CO_2 per mile (394 g/km) and travels only

Buses and streetcars compete with cars in Hong Kong. Good public transportation is vital in modern cities, with integrated systems linking road travel with overland and underground trains. If the system is efficient, more people will be able to leave their cars at home.

17 miles per gallon (6 km/l). In Great Britain and many other countries, road taxes are higher for drivers of cars that produce more pollution. Considering the fact that at least 44 million cars are manufactured throughout the world every year, it is clearly important to reduce the amount of CO_2 that they emit.

Biofuels and Hybrids

One way to replace fossil fuels is to run cars on fuel from biomass, an energy source that includes all plant matter and animal waste that produce usable gases in landfill sites and sewage plants. The carbon dioxide released by burning biomass is no greater than the amount that was taken in by the growing plants. Also, the crops planted for use as fuel biomass will absorb the carbon dioxide the burning plants produce. This closed carbon cycle makes biomass a carbon-neutral resource. It does not increase the overall amount of CO_2 in the atmosphere, although trucks that transport it many miles may add to the CO_2 emissions. In Brazil, sugarcane is used as a source of fuel, and most new Brazilian cars are capable of running on pure ethanol (also called E-100). Ethanol can also be made from other grasses such as corn and barley or from plants such as sugar beets or potatoes. Pure or blended biodiesel can be produced by extracting oil from soybeans, rapeseed, or peanuts.

Another option is the hybrid car, which combines a gasoline, diesel, or biofuel engine with an electric motor that takes over at low speeds. The action of the brakes recharges the battery for the electric motor. Honda, Toyota, and other car manufacturers are increasing their sales of hybrids.

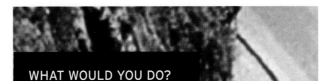

WHAT WOULD YOU DO?

You Are in Charge
You work for an international travel company that has to raise its prices to pay for higher air costs and carbon taxes. How would you explain the increases to customers?

Fuel Cells

Hydrogen gas can be used to generate electricity and power cars. Hydrogen fuel cells convert chemical energy to electrical energy by combining hydrogen and oxygen. One drawback is that the energy needed to make the hydrogen often comes from a fossil fuel that emits CO_2. However, hydrogen could be made from water using electricity generated from renewable sources.

CHAPTER 8

What Can We Do?

It is September 2020, and members of an environmental group are meeting at an eco-village. The residents of the village use solar panels and wind turbines to create their own energy, and they recycle everything that they can. They and their guests know that lifestyle changes will not be enough to limit climate change due to global warming during the rest of the twenty-first century. They discuss other ways to slow down and stabilize climate change and draw up an action plan to convince politicians that new agreements are necessary. The Tokyo meeting in March this year was a start, but these environmentalists believe that more action is urgently needed.

One of the most obvious ways in which we can avoid making the situation worse is to stop pumping so much carbon dioxide into Earth's atmosphere. Limiting this activity is not easy when experts say that the demand for electricity, for example, will nearly double by 2030. Currently, about one-third of primary energy goes to generate electricity. Most electricity is produced by burning fossil fuels. We could, however, use renewable sources to satisfy more of our energy needs, and promising developments have come along in the use of hydroelectric, biomass, solar, wind, geothermal, tidal, and wave power.

Energy Mix

Some experts think that renewable sources will never be enough and that without fossil fuels we could be

PROJECTED USE OF RENEWABLE ENERGY

	Year 1990 %	Year 2020 %
Traditional Biomass (woodfuels, etc.)	10.6	9.3
Hydro (water)	5.3	5.8
Modern Biomass (biofuels, waste, etc.)	1.4	5.0
Solar	0.1	3.1
Wind	0.0	1.9
Geothermal (Earth's heat)	0.1	0.8
Micro-hydro (small water generators)	0.2	0.6
Tidal and wave	0.0	0.5
TOTAL	17.7	27.0

Source: World Energy Council

left with an energy gap. Another alternative—nuclear power is not a renewable resource, because nuclear fuel (from the mined radioactive metal uranium) is used up to produce power. One of the big advantages of nuclear power, however, is that it produces a huge amount of energy from a small amount of fuel. Another advantage that is very important when considering global warming is that nuclear processes do not release carbon dioxide. Using nuclear power has big disadvantages, however, including the problems of nuclear waste and possible accidents at nuclear power stations. Other concerns include the possibility that terrorists might obtain nuclear material and use it for the wrong purpose.

The many and varied advantages and disadvantages of different energy sources lead many people to believe that we should be looking for a good mix instead of totally excluding any one of them.

Small and Self-Sufficient

Another way forward is to use more microsystems, in which individual homes or communities have their own wind turbine, solar panels, or water turbine. Many countries have programs to help people with the costs of installing these microgenerators. In Spain, for example, all new homes must now have solar panels built into their roofs. Individuals can still be connected to the national electricity grid in case their microgenerators do not consistently provide enough energy. Another incentive to having a private microsystem is that if the microsystem is so successful that it produces more electricity than your household or community needs, you can sell any surplus electricity to the national grid for others to use.

This energy-efficient house in California has a turf roof for insulation and solar panels to provide electricity.

International Agreements

By the terms of the Kyoto Protocol, the developed and industrialized countries of the world agreed that by the year 2012, they would reduce their emissions of greenhouse gases by at least 5.2 percent of their 1990 levels. That figure would be a reduction of about 29 percent on the emissions that might otherwise occur by then. According to the UN, reductions of only 3.5 percent had been made by early 2006.

One problem with this international agreement is that it has not been ratified by Australia or by the world's biggest emitter of CO_2,

A demonstrator shows his support for the UN Climate Change Conference in Montréal, Canada, in 2005. Conference delegates looked ahead to what their countries could do to limit global warming after 2012.

the United States. The United States produced 6,435 million tons (5,838 million tonnes) of CO_2 in 2002—almost one-quarter of the world's total, while Australia produced 392 million tons (356 million tonnes) of CO_2 .

The top five emitters of CO_2 are the United States (24.3%), China (14.5%), Russia (5.9%), India (5.1%), and Japan (5.0%). The Kyoto agreement classifies both China and India as developing countries, which means that they are not required to make reductions by 2012. Both countries have rapidly growing economies and vast populations, however, and will therefore produce and use more energy. It is likely that the international community will want to change China's and India's classification when they agree what is to happen by 2020.

The governments of some countries, particularly the United States, are concerned that a reduction in energy use will harm their economy and make unemployment worse. They are also worried that less use of fossil fuels will leave them with an energy gap that renewable sources cannot fill. Experts say, however, that renewable sources could be much more efficient than they currently are if more research and development were put into them now.

WHAT WOULD YOU DO?

You Are in Charge
You are a government official looking into the use of energy resources. Which of these sources would you choose to develop:

■ fossil fuels (oil, gas, coal)
■ nuclear energy
■ renewable sources (biomass, solar, wind, geothermal, hydroelectric)

Individual responsibility

Although as individuals we cannot stop the polar ice caps from melting or the seas from rising, we can all help in our own way to reduce greenhouse gas emissions. We can use energy more wisely and efficiently by switching off lights when we leave the room and not leaving electrical appliances such as computers on when we are not using them. We can also travel more sensibly, sharing cars so that we save fuel, using public transportation and energy-efficient vehicles, and especially by walking or bicycling whenever possible.

All the measures that international communities and individuals take can make a difference to global warming. If we were to do nothing, the situation would undoubtedly be more difficult by 2020. That would leave the responsibility—and the problems—to future generations. We must all take responsibility now.

Glossary

afforestation The conversion of land into forest by planting new trees

albedo effect The capacity of a surface to reflect the Sun's warmth and light; snow and ice have a high albedo; brown earth has a low albedo

atoll A ring-shaped series of coral islands surrounding a shallow lagoon

biodiversity The variety of plant and animal life in the world or in a particular habitat or region

biofuel A fuel produced from biomass

biomass All plant and animal matter

carbon cycle The series of interlinked processes on Earth by which carbon compounds are exchanged between living things and the atmosphere

climate The general weather conditions in an area over a long period of time

climatologist A scientist who studies climate

coelenterate An animal in a family of sea animals that includes corals, jellyfishes, and sea anemones

deficit The amount by which something is too small (such as production compared with consumption)

deforestation The cutting down and removal of forest trees

delta The area near the mouth of some rivers, where the flow splits into several different channels

desertification The process by which fertile dry land becomes desert

ecosystem A group of living things that are dependent on each other and their environment

El Niño Periodic changes in winds and currents of the Pacific Ocean that bring extreme weather to countries around the ocean; see also ENSO

emission The process of emitting, or producing and giving off, something such as a gas

ENSO (El Niño–Southern Oscillation) The cycle of changes between El Niño, normal, and La Niña conditions in the Pacific region

environmentalist A person who is concerned about and acts to protect the natural environment

fossil fuel A fuel (such as coal, oil and natural gas) that comes from the fossilized remains of prehistoric plants and animals; fossil fuels are nonrenewable

geothermal The heat from within the Earth

glacier A slowly-moving mass or river of ice formed by compacted snow on high ground

greenhouse effect The warming of the Earth's surface by the natural effect of a blanket of certain gases in the atmosphere; the effect is increased by gases such as carbon dioxide emitted by human activity, especially from burning fossil fuels

greenhouse gas A gas, such as carbon dioxide, that traps heat from the Sun near Earth and helps create the greenhouse effect

groundwater Water held underground in porous rocks

hydroelectricity Electricity generated by moving water, especially from a dam across a river

ice age Any of the periods in history when there were ice sheets across large parts of Earth's surface

ice cap A covering of ice over a large area

ice sheet A thick layer of ice over a large area that remains frozen for a long period

ice shelf A floating sheet of ice that is attached to coastal land

indigenous people The original or native people of a region

interglacial period A period between ice ages

irrigate To water land in order to help crops to grow

La Niña Changes in the Pacific Ocean that bring cold water to the surface; see also ENSO

levee An embankment built to stop flooding

meteorologist A scientist who studies and forecasts the weather

ozone layer A layer of ozone gas high in the Earth's atmosphere that absorbs most ultraviolet radiation from the Sun

pack ice A mass of ice floating on the sea

permafrost Ground in the polar regions that remains permanently frozen.

polder An area of land reclaimed from the sea and protected by embankments

pollute To damage (the environment, atmosphere, etc.) with harmful substances

primary energy The energy available in a natural energy source (such as coal or sunlight) before it is changed into motor power or electricity; some of the primary energy is wasted during the change to another form of power

protocol A formal agreement between nations

ratify To approve something formally so that it comes into effect

renewable energy A source of energy that does not run out by being used, such as water, wind, solar, or geothermal power; the term includes sources that can be replaced, such as biomass

summit A meeting between heads of government to discuss important international matters

tsunami Huge destructive waves caused by an undersea earthquake

wetland Land, such as marshes or swamps, that is saturated or covered with water for most of the time

wildfire A fierce fire that spreads rapidly, especially a forest fire

Further Information

Books

Arthus-Bertrand, Yann. *The Future of the Earth: An Introduction to Sustainable Development for Young Readers.* Harry Abrams 2004.

Pringle, Laurence. *Global Warming: The Threat of Earth's Changing Climate.* Seastar 2001.

Scoones, Simon. *Climate Change: Our Impact on the Planet.* Hodder Wayland, 2004.

Web Sites

www.climateprediction.net
BBC Climate Change Experiment
Use your computer to join in the largest climate prediction experiment ever, developed by climatologists using the Meteorological Office climate model.

www.greenpeace.org/international
Greenpeace International
Interesting practical information from the global environmental organization that looks for solutions and alternatives. Greenpeace campaigns for the "phasing-out of fossil fuels and the promotion of renewable energies in order to stop climate change."

www.ipcc.ch
The Intergovernmental Panel on Climate Change
This site assesses all information concerning the scientific basis of risk of human-induced climate change. A very informative Web site with the latest technical information and statistics.

epa.gov/climatechange/index.html
Environmental Protection Agency's Global Warming Site
Information on global warming from the US Environmental Protection Agency, including a section on "Individuals can make a difference."

Publisher's note to educators and parents: Our editors have carefully reviewed these Web sites to ensure that they are suitable for children. Many Web sites change frequently, however, and we cannot guarantee that a site's future contents will continue to meet our high standards of quality and educational value. Be advised that children should be closely supervised whenever they access the Internet.

What Would You Do?

Page 7:
All five measures are important, so it is difficult to put them in order of priority. Most experts think that the most important step is to reduce CO_2 emissions; all the other actions would help achieve this goal.

Page 13:
You could concentrate on how the changing environment will affect local people's lives. You might want to focus on ways in which a traditional way of life can be combined with modern progress. You could use figures from these pages or more local statistics for your community, perhaps from the Arctic Council. The council concentrates on environmental, social, and economic issues.

Page 18:
You might argue that all nations should be accountable, but that the biggest emitters of CO_2—the United States and the European Union as a group—should pay most to help those who cannot afford to help themselves.

Page 25:
You could reply that many scientists believe that global warming will lead to big changes in water supplies, including rivers. The situation, however, is complicated by many other factors, such as land management. Your local scientists, engineers, and politicians will need to take all these into consideration when reviewing plans for the dam.

Page 31:
Here are just some examples: Governments and politicians could monitor logging more closely and prosecute illegal loggers. Publishers could use recycled and so-called forest-friendly paper for their books (many do this already, but not all). We can all look carefully at the wood (such as furniture) that we buy; it should be certified by the Forest Stewardship Council (FSC).

Page 34:
The WMO conducts climate research that, it says, provides vital information for advance warnings that save lives and reduce damage to property and the environment. You could quote this and use the ability to predict such events as droughts or El Niños as possible examples.

Page 41:
You could mention the concerns about the greenhouse effect and global warming. You could also encourage your company to produce an informational leaflet, which has the advantage of showing that it cares for the environment as well as for its customers.

Page 45:
Some countries have an energy policy based on all available energy sources. To limit greenhouse gases, renewable sources are best. Some countries, such as France, favor nuclear power stations, but these present huge problems such as radioactive waste disposal. Fossil fuels are worst for global warming and will not last forever. You might suggest a mix with the priority on renewable sources.

Index